LEARN ABOUT VALUES

PATRIOTISM

by Cynthia Roberts

Published in the United States of America by The Child's World®
1980 Lookout Drive • Mankato, MN 56003-1705 • 800-599-READ • www.childsworld.com

The Child's World®: Mary Berendes, Publishing Director; Katherine Stevenson, Editor
The Design Lab: Kathy Petelinsek, Art Director; Julia Goozen, Design and Page Production

Photo Credits: © Anatoly Maltsev/epa/Corbis: 15; © AP Photo/Roberto Candia: 11; © David M. Budd Photography: 5, 7, 13; © Gabe
Palmer/Corbis: 19; © John Henley/Corbis: cover; © John W. Gertz/zefa/Corbis: 17; © Kevin Dodge/Corbis: 21; © SCPhotos/Alamy: 9

Library of Congress Cataloging-in-Publication Data
Roberts, Cynthia, 1960–
    Patriotism / by Cynthia Roberts.
       p. cm. — (Learn about values)
    ISBN 978-1-59296-674-5 ISBN 1-59296-674-8 (library bound : alk. paper)
    1. Patriotism—Juvenile literature.   I. Title. II. Series.
  JC329.R64 2006
    323.6'5—dc22   2006000962

CONTENTS

What Is Patriotism?

Patriotism is a feeling of love and respect for your country. There are lots of different countries in the world. Most people love the land in which they live. They are proud of it. They show their patriotism in many different ways.

These American children are showing their patriotism.

Patriotism **in Words**

People often put their feelings of patriotism into words. They might write poems about their country. They might talk about the beauty of their land. Or they might write about its past. They might talk about making it a better place. They might make a **pledge** to keep it safe.

In the U.S., schoolchildren often say the Pledge of **Allegiance**.

Patriotism and Flags

Each country has its own flag. The flag is a **symbol** for the country.
Flags come in all colors and patterns. The colors and patterns stand
for different things. People are proud of their countries' flags. They
fly them to show their patriotism.

This is the United Nations building. These flags belong to some of the nations that meet here.

Patriotism **and Music**

People often write or play music to honor their countries. Often the music has words. Sometimes it does not. Each country has its own **anthem**. An anthem is a special song that honors the country. The anthem of the U.S. is "The Star-Spangled Banner."

These Brazilian soccer players are singing their national anthem.

11

Patriotism and Parades

People often show patriotism in parades. They carry their nation's flags. Sometimes they wear their nation's colors. Many countries hold parades on special days. Often these are days when important things happened in the country's past.

In the U.S., people often hold parades on the Fourth of July. This holiday honors the nation's beginnings.

Patriotism and Voting

Many countries hold **elections** to choose their leaders. People vote for the person they think will do the best job. The person who gets the most votes wins. Voting gives everyone a say in how things should be done. It is a special way of showing patriotism.

This woman is from Belarus. She is voting to choose her nation's leaders.

Keeping Countries Safe

Some people have special jobs keeping their countries safe. Many of them serve in the **military**. They try to keep the nation from being attacked. If they need to, they fight for their land. Many people show their patriotism by doing this job.

This American man has promised to protect his country.

17

Patriotism **and You**

How can you show patriotism? Learning about your country is a great place to start! You can learn about your nation's past. You can learn about its land and people. You can learn how its **government** works. You can learn what problems it faces today. You can think about how to make it better.

Schoolchildren all over the world learn about their own countries.

19

Patriotism Makes Countries Stronger

People everywhere want good places to live. They have different ideas about what their countries should be like. But they show patriotism by doing their part. They work to make their countries better and stronger.

Your country is a big part of who you are.

glossary

allegiance
To show allegiance is to support something and stand by it.

anthem
An anthem is a national song.

elections
In elections, people vote to pick their leaders.

government
A government is a group of people in charge of running a country.

military
A country's military is its army of people who are ready to fight for it.

pledge
A pledge is a promise.

symbol
A symbol is something that stands for something else.

books

Lamachia, John. *So What Is Patriotism Anyway?* New York: Rosen, 1999.

Webster, Christine. *The Pledge of Allegiance* (Cornerstones of Freedom, second series). Chicago: Children's Press, 2003.

Whipple, Wayne. *The Story of the American Flag.* Bedford, MA: Applewood Books, 2000.

web sites

Visit our Web page for links about character education and values:
http://www.childsworld.com/links

Note to parents, teachers, and librarians:
We routinely check our Web links to make sure they're safe, active sites—so encourage your readers to check them out!

index

about the author

Even as a child, Cynthia Roberts knew she wanted to be a writer. She is always working to involve kids in reading and writing, and she loves spending time in the children's section of the library or bookstore. Cynthia enjoys gardening, traveling, and having fun with friends and family.